DEGREE APPRENTICESHIP APPLICATION GUIDE

ABOUT THIS BOOK

Gain a degree while being paid and make a fast start to your career? Degree apprenticeships have become an exciting option for when you leave school. How can you develop the skills to compete? How can you explore all your options to ensure you have choices?

Written for you by a leading careers professional, this book tells you where to look, how to apply and how to present yourself. You will hear too from leading employers about how they recruit talent like yours and current apprentices will give you an idea of what it's like being a degree apprentice.

AUTHOR

Frances Trought is the founder of Everything D&I (EDI), creators of opportunities for diverse talent with a focus on race, gender and social mobility. Talent is everywhere and EDI aims to ensure opportunity is too.

Frances has worked with industry leaders, including Accenture, Microsoft and Rolls-Royce, to develop innovative initiatives to create a sense of belonging and awareness of career opportunities. Frances is the author of *Brilliant Employability Skills* and provides a blend of coaching and mentoring to support others on their journey to career success.

DEGREE APPRENTICESHIP APPLICATION GUIDE

HOW TO PREPARE AND APPLY FOR DEGREE APPRENTICESHIPS

FRANCES TROUGHT

FEATURING ACCENTURE, MICROSOFT AND ROLLS-ROYCE

**Degree Apprenticeship Application Guide:
How to prepare and apply for degree apprenticeships**

Every possible effort has been made to ensure that the information contained in this publication is accurate at the time of going to press. Neither the publisher nor the authors can accept responsibility for any errors or omissions, however caused. Nor can any responsibility be accepted for loss or damage as a result of reading this publication.

Published by Novaro Publishing Ltd, 2 Speedwell Drive, Lindfield, West Sussex e: publish@novaropublishing.com.

© Everything D&I Ltd, 2024

The right of Frances Trought to be identified as the author of this publication has been asserted by her in accordance with the Copyright, Design and Patents Act 1988.

All rights reserved. Apart from any fair dealing for the purposes of research or private study, criticism or review, this publication may only be reproduced, stored or transmitted in any form or by any means with the prior permission in writing of the publisher.

ISBN: 978-1-7398640-8-8

A CIP catalogue record for this book is available from the British Library.

Designed by Chantel Barnett, Clear Design CC Ltd.

For further details about our authors and our titles, see www.novaropublishing.com.

Dedicated to all the young talent navigating their way through degree apprenticeships. Go shine your light.

ACKNOWLEDGEMENTS

Thank you to everyone who made this guide possible:

Andy Coker
Carol Parillon
Carrie Brodie
Corinne Ferguson
Damian Corneal
Diahann Abraham
Ellie Long
Ivy Kayima
Jezneel Durogene
Jorrell Trought
Karen Kufuor
Magdalena Kotska
Melodie Trought
Michael Rene
Stella Mosley
Symphonie Trought
Veslyn Mclean

CONTENTS

Foreword
*Damian Corneal, partner, PwC and vice chair,
London Apprenticeship Ambassador Network*   ix

Preface   xiii
Introduction   1

Part 1: Becoming an apprentice
1. Degree apprenticeships defined   9
2. Finding opportunities   23
3. Preparing to compete   30
4. Your CV   38
5. Interviews and assessments   47

Part 2: Employer profiles
6. Accenture   61
7. Microsoft   84
8. Rolls-Royce   102

Conclusion   124

Sources   125

FOREWORD

Apprenticeships as a means of mastering a profession is not a new concept; they have in fact existed for centuries. Modern-day apprenticeships and the employer-driven standards that underpin them have evolved to the point where they are an equivalent route into employment. Many students even see them as preferential to pursuing a purely academic degree prior to seeking an entry-level position. However, the historical legacy of apprenticeships being perceived as only for trades and craftsmen, or for those less academically inclined, has led to some ingrained misunderstandings around who they are for and the benefits they now provide. This guide aims to demystify the misconceptions about apprenticeships for schools, parents, carers and students.

Over a decade ago, I began my personal journey as an ambassador for apprenticeships within a large technology consulting firm. Our apprenticeship programme was initiated with a strong business case and clear economic drivers. We needed to expand the pool of talent we attracted and in the fast-paced world of technology, required a breadth of ever-evolving skills, knowledge and behaviours that could not be solely provided by universities.

What became quickly apparent was twofold; the positive attitude and aptitude of the apprentices to learn the in-demand skills needed, coupled with our ability to shape their ways of working and culture, provided cohorts of high-quality talent in a relatively short time frame. More importantly, we witnessed first hand the transformational impact the programme had on individual apprentices, their families and their communities.

The game-changing impact of apprenticeships was especially noticeable for those from under-represented and lower socioeconomic backgrounds. Over the years I've seen many apprentices who started on the level-3 apprenticeship (A-level equivalent) or on the degree apprenticeship programmes, go on to be the first in their family to attain a degree qualification. This was achieved while earning to support their families, graduating with no student debt and with guaranteed full-time employment. These apprentices are thriving in companies that previously they would not have even thought of or been able to apply to. Having had the privilege of being a judge for both the National Apprenticeship Awards and the Multicultural

FOREWORD

Apprenticeship Awards, I have seen similar inspirational stories across industries, organisations and communities throughout our nation.

With all these positives, the support of government initiatives and the recognised value that apprenticeships bring in the business community, why do we need this guide? Because even though apprenticeships can be transformational in the lives of our under-represented young people, only 10 percent of apprenticeship starts for 16 to 18-year-olds are from under-represented backgrounds. Based on conversations with other employers, training providers, parents and students over the years, this predominantly stems from a lack of awareness about what modern apprenticeships offer, lack of information for students in schools and the overwhelming pressure placed on them to pursue a traditional university path. This is why we need this guide – to bridge the awareness gap and to empower teachers, parents and students.

I've previously worked with Everything D&I (EDI) on many diversity and inclusion initiatives, and know they similarly recognise this apprenticeship awareness gap and the resultant missed opportunities for students. With a track record in bringing industry and educators together to provide opportunities for students from diverse backgrounds, EDI is well positioned to support schools in driving apprenticeship awareness. They have collaborated with several large employers including Microsoft, Rolls-Royce and Accenture in the production of this guide. Most employers, including PwC, truly recognise the value in building a diverse pipeline of talent, generally and through the apprenticeship route.

We collectively and urgently need to shift the narrative from 'apprenticeships are for those who do not achieve grades for university' to 'apprenticeships are for those who want to master their profession through doing, learning on the job from colleagues with vast experience, and adopting the latest industry developments in real time'. All without the financial burden or employment uncertainty following university graduation. This guide will empower schools and parents with the information they need to help future generations make fully informed choices, with the broadest view of the opportunities available, to achieve both their professional and academic aspirations.

Damian Corneal, partner, PwC and vice chair, London Apprenticeship Ambassador Network

PREFACE

At Everything D&I, the objective is to create opportunities for diverse talent with a focus on race, gender and social mobility. Our aim is to ensure that students regardless of their background are able to successfully engage in the process of being selected for degree apprenticeships. During our work with students in secondary schools, sixth forms and colleges there are varying levels of awareness of the kind of degree apprenticeships available, but a limited understanding of the selection process. Many students had not participated in a competitive application process, not even for part-time work, and so this was their first formal interview. As a result, the readiness to compete varies significantly across schools. The purpose of this guide is to bridge that gap and ensure that students are able to prepare before the application season and develop the skills needed to compete, opening up their options beyond the traditional route of applying to university. We want to ensure that

PREFACE

students have all the information to make the right choice for them between degree apprenticeships and university.

Frances Trought
Founder, Everything D&I

INTRODUCTION

Success is often defined as going to university and many of you will hear this at family gatherings, at school and amongst friends. This is particularly true for students, who are the first generation in their family to have the opportunity to attend university. Attending university is a proud moment for families. It is seen as a gateway to better careers, increased income and a kickstart to better life options.

Degree apprenticeships have disrupted this model in every way. They present an alternative path to success with the ability to secure a degree and a career with no debt.

Many parents, schools and students remain to be convinced. In our survey of students, we found that many schools would not present high-performing students with the option for degree apprenticeships. There is still an element of scepticism. The awareness of the benefits of degree apprenticeships has increased significantly with 40 percent of applicants, a total of approximately 500,000, were interested in degree apprenticeships (University and College Admissions Service, 2024). There are still a vast proportion of students and parents, who are unaware.

The degree apprenticeship process is less established and searching for opportunities is not centralised, although UCAS and the government are working towards this. At present, opportunities can be found on the UK government's apprenticeship portal, as well as on company websites.

The dates for applications vary from opening at the beginning of year 13 and running all the way through to June. The process of applying is also varied; some requiring CVs, others have their own application forms. Unlike university, when everyone prepares one personal statement, a single process has yet to be established for degree apprenticeships. These variations can cause confusion, as there is no central point of reference. It can be challenging to not only find opportunities, but also to prepare to compete. Students from under-represented groups and lower socioeconomic backgrounds often have the grades, but need support in making it through the processes of application and selection.

The process of applying for university is firmly embedded within the school timetable. There is a clear cycle of activity to ensure that students complete the tasks needed to

INTRODUCTION

compete for university. Schools aim to submit their UCAS applications in the January of year 13. Schools assign time for the development of the personal statement and actively encourage students to review university degree options.

Teachers and careers advisers provide checks and references, encouraging students to explore their interests, strengths and career aspirations to support their application. Universities give them the opportunity to explore courses through invitations to attend open days and virtual tours, as well as speaking to current students.

It is a well-established cycle that happens every year, so students know what deadlines to expect. Similarly, it is clear what is involved in preparing a personal statement and what type of content can it make stand out. Even within the academic year, there are activities to ensure that all students are working towards this aim.

Degree apprenticeships were introduced in 2015, but the path is less defined, increasingly competitive and more fragmented. Students can apply via UCAS but also directly to companies and the deadlines are scattered throughout the year.

For a student entering into year 13, it can be confusing and frustrating. UCAS and the government are currently working together to provide more opportunities on the UCAS platform.

Despite these efforts, it does not address the issue of how students can best compete. The number of places for degree apprenticeships varies. Companies may have 8 or 40 places available, but receive thousands of applications. The support provided to students at home, at school or from the careers advice can vary significantly. What does a competitive CV look like? What does it mean to be competitive in an interview and how do you prepare?

At EDI, we run a programme to support applications for degree apprenticeships. Levels of the students vary. Even though they are on track to secure As, Bs and Cs in their A-levels, they are not ready to apply for degree apprenticeships. This is how this guide came about, because we found many students unaware of how competitive the process is.

Although applying to university is competitive, there is only a need to submit one application. For degree apprenticeships, you compete in each company's process, so it can involve several rounds engaging in interviews, tests and presentations. All too often, students are not ready for this rigorous process and find it challenging.

A well-resourced school will help students to write a competitive CV, prepare them for interviews and support them throughout the process. In our experience the support for degree apprenticeships is increasing within schools,

INTRODUCTION

but what is becoming apparent is that there's a lack of understanding of how apprentices are actually selected.

Teachers and careers advisors are well versed in what a good personal statement looks like and what it should contain, but there is a lack of understanding of what is a good CV and how to prepare for the psychometric tests, interviews and assessment centres within each company.

The aim of this guide is to try and close that gap to provide some guidance with regards to where to find opportunities, how to prepare and how to compete. The guide also enlists the help of Accenture, Microsoft and Rolls-Royce to provide some insights into their selection processes, which will be useful regardless of which degree apprenticeship you apply for.

Whether you are a student applying for degree apprenticeships, a parent trying to support your young adult, or a careers advisor or teacher trying to help your students plan their future, this guide has something for you.

PART 1

BECOMING AN APPRENTICE

1.
DEGREE APPRENTICESHIPS DEFINED

Differences and similarities between degree apprenticeships and university degrees

A degree apprenticeship, as defined by the Office for Students, 'is a particular type of job, which combines work with higher-level learning, and which leads to an undergraduate or postgraduate degree'.

A degree apprenticeship allows you to combine studying for a degree with on-the-job learning. Students will benefit from a salary, work experience and payment of university fees by their employer.

Degree apprenticeships are available in a number of industries with degrees from a range of disciplines ranging from law to technology. There is something for everyone, as they come with varying entry requirements and range of degree options to different universities. Each company will have partnered with a university as a learning provider to deliver the degree element of the programme. Its delivery can also vary:

- **Online**: the degree is delivered virtually via online classes.

- **In person**: degree apprentices travel to the university campus one day a week

- **Block**: as the name suggests teaching is delivered in blocks of three to ten weeks, enabling students to gain a fast-track insight into the role and skills required.

- **Semester**: apprentices attend university alongside other university students and commit to a ten-week placement in the summer and a twelve-month placement in the third year of their degree.

Companies have partnered with universities across the entire university league table, hence the different levels of UCAS points required for the various programmes. When choosing a degree apprenticeship, there is often not the opportunity to choose which university you attend; the company will have already selected a partner university.

As a result, students should enquire about how the degree will be delivered to ensure it suits their learning style. There should be a focus on the skills and experience you gain as part of the degree apprenticeship and the opportunity to gain regular experience with a global organisation.

How and where will you work?

When applying for degree apprenticeships, it is important to also understand the nature of the work. For example: is it hybrid, ie, two days in the office and three days at home? does the role involve travel? will you need to relocate? Although you should not let this deter you, it is good to be aware. Do remember that if you have chosen a degree apprenticeship outside of travelling distance from your home and you are required to relocate, this is the same as leaving home for university. Your first year of university may involve you relocating and finding accommodation. Often other apprentices will also relocate, so you could find yourself living in a flat with them. If you decide to leave home, you will cover your rent out of your salary and will not have access to student loans.

Salary and benefits

As a degree apprentice you will receive a salary. The amount varies for each programme, but on average you can expect to start on between £14,000 and £27,000 depending on the company. This money does not need to be repaid and is your reward for the work you do. Some companies will also offer you a sign-on bonus, a reward for joining their organisation. This can range from £500 to £1000.

By joining as a degree apprentice, you become an employee and so you are also eligible for other staff benefits including healthcare, pensions, gym memberships, life insurance, cycle-to-work schemes etc. Each company will have a range of benefits.

University fees

All university fees will be paid by your employer, unlike the traditional university student, who is financed by student loans. It is an essential point about degree apprenticeships.

Duration

Degree apprenticeships will range in length and take from three to six years to complete. Three years is the most usual in line with the majority of university degrees. Apprentices can expect pay rises and, on completion, are often offered a contract of employment beyond the apprenticeship. The latest report from the Department for Business, Innovation, and Skills, states that 90 percent of apprentices are offered permanent employment either during their apprenticeship or on graduation. Students can also command a higher salary in the graduate job market, as they will have three years' experience, as well as a degree.

Who can apply for a degree apprenticeship?

Degree apprenticeships are open to young adults of all ages, but are particular targeted as an alternative to attending university for 18-year-old school leavers, who have completed a level-3 qualification (A-levels, BTEC, T-levels). Applicants will also usually have secured five GCSEs with grades 9-4, including English language and mathematics. Depending on the programme you apply for, there may be other requirements. For instance, an engineering degree apprenticeship may stipulate that you have studied mathematics at A-level and require a minimum of a 5 in mathematics at GCSE. As a result, it is useful to research your options as early as possible to ensure you are making the right A-level choices and select opportunities in line with your academic achievements.

Degree apprenticeships v university

There is no right or wrong answer. If students choose to attend university or apply for a degree apprenticeship, it is about ensuring that they are aware of the choices available. Each option is valid, so it is important to ensure students keep their options open. Ensure you have choices when results day comes around. Below is a table outlining the differences and similarities between degree apprenticeships and universities.

	Degree apprenticeship	**University degree**
Differences and similarities	Degree apprenticeships can be found via the University and Colleges Admission Service (UCAS) or on the company website. There is no one designated place to find all of the degree apprenticeship opportunities.	All degree courses are listed on the UCAS website, as well as some apprenticeships, including all levels.

DEFINED

	Degree apprenticeship	**University degree**
Insight days and open days	Companies will hold both in-person and virtual insight days for candidates to learn more about their opportunities. To attend, register on their website to receive notifications.	Register on university websites for the relevant course to receive notifications of open days and virtual campus tours.
Open	Degree apprenticeships open at various times during year 13. Register on sites so they can notify you when the applications open.	Students generally start to submit applications towards the end of the autumn term. Every school has clear timelines for when students will begin to prepare and submit their university applications.

DEGREE APPRENTICESHIP APPLICATION GUIDE

	Degree apprenticeship	**University degree**
Deadline	Various deadlines depend on the company. Do not wait for the deadline to apply as many applications will close before the deadline.	Students will submit applications in January of year 13.
Application	All applicants will need to submit an application to the company of their choice. Each application process will vary, so students need to develop a tailored response to each company.	Students will develop a personal statement and UCAS will distribute this statement to your five university choices. These choices may include degree apprenticeships for companies that promote their opportunities through UCAS.

	Degree apprenticeship	**University degree**
Number of applications	Students can apply for an unlimited number of companies. They are not limited in the number of companies they can submit applications to, but they will need to ensure they have the required grades. The selection process can involve three or four stages over several months, so students must balance their applications with their academic studies.	UCAS offers candidates five options which can be a mixture of university choices and degree apprenticeships advertised via the platform. Students will then receive offers, based on their predicted grades. Very few universities require students to complete interviews, so once the personal statement is submitted, students can simply await the outcome of their application.

DEGREE APPRENTICESHIP APPLICATION GUIDE

	Degree apprenticeship	**University degree**
Selection process	Each company will have its own selection process, so you will undergo a selection process for each company that reflects its values and behaviours.	Universities will assess your personal statement and predicted grades to decide if they will make you an offer subject to the attainment of your grades in the summer.
Location	Degree apprenticeships are on offer throughout the UK, so you are not limited to companies within travelling distance.	Universities degrees are available throughout the UK with universities providing a range of experiences.
Delivery	Students can expect to work for four days and spend the fifth day studying. Many companies also operate hybrid	University is delivered in two semesters ranging from 10-12 weeks. Your timetable will usually be delivered across

DEFINED

	Degree apprenticeship	University degree
Delivery (continued)	working, so apprentices can expect to work one or two days from home. Degree apprenticeships can also be delivered where you study for the academic year at university and then work for the company in the summer months. Be sure to ask how the programme will be delivered.	three days, but some courses are five days a week. Teaching will be delivered in person with a mixture of lectures (large classes delivered in lecture halls with often more than a hundred students) and seminars (delivered in small groups ranging from 10-25).
Start dates	Degree apprenticeships tend to begin the September after you finish year 13 and receive your summer exam results.	University will commence mid-September / October.

DEGREE APPRENTICESHIP APPLICATION GUIDE

	Degree apprenticeship	**University degree**
Holiday periods	Companies will provide about 20-30 days holidays plus any bank holidays.	Universities allow extended breaks at Christmas (3-5 weeks), Easter (3-5 weeks) and summer (12-14 weeks).
Work experience	Work experience is inbuilt into the degree apprentice and often the apprentices are recruited upon completion of their course.	University students have to compete every year to secure work experience. Upon graduation there is no guarantee of a job. There is no guarantee that you will secure work experience upon completion of your degree.
University fees	All of your university fees are paid for by your employer. Each year they will pay the degree	At university, every year you will apply for your student loans to meet your university fees. The funds will be

DEFINED

	Degree apprenticeship	**University degree**
University fees (continued)	fees. There is no requirement to pay the fees back, as they are included in your degree apprenticeship.	paid directly to the university and you will begin to repay the fees on completion of your degree dependent on your salary (gov.uk/repaying-your-student-loan).
Salary v maintenance loan	As a degree apprentice you will earn a salary, which ranges from £14,000 to £27,000. There is no requirement to pay it back.	As a university student you will apply for a maintenance loan up to £13,000, depending upon the university you attend, your parents' income and if you remain at home or move to student accommodation. You will apply for a loan for each year of your degree, and you are not liable to start

	Degree apprenticeship	**University degree**
Salary v maintenance loan (continued)		repaying the loan upon graduation (gov.uk/student-finance/new-fulltime-students).
Graduate jobs	On completion of the degree apprenticeship, most companies offer apprentices a graduate role.	On completion of the degree, there are no guarantees of securing a graduate role.

Summary

Degree apprenticeships are a viable alternative to traditional university. As with all career decisions, it is important to do your research and weigh up your options. To ensure awareness of both the university and degree apprenticeship experience attend university open days and company insight events. Watch videos of current apprentices and university students. Use the insights and research to guide your decision-making.

2.
FINDING DEGREE APPRENTICESHIP OPPORTUNITIES

Ten steps for finding a degree apprenticeship programme

The number of companies offering degree apprenticeships is increasing every year alongside the options available. One of the most recent is the option to become a medical doctor, which is a game changer in the medical profession.

It is important to start your search early. Begin searching for programmes of interest and the entry requirements. The process of searching for the right degree apprenticeship requires the same energy as searching for a traditional university course. Below are ten steps to finding a degree apprenticeship programme.

1) What are your career interests?

You may already know what career you want to pursue, so this step does not apply to you. If you are, like many students, unsure what career you want to pursue, begin by reflecting on your subjects. What do you like about your current areas of study? You may also want to think about passions that you are not currently studying. For instance, you may have a passion for tech, but are studying humanities. Find what interests you. There may be more areas than one.

2) Register on platforms

Finding an opportunity for a degree apprenticeship is not as straightforward as finding a degree course. Opportunities are marketed directly on company websites, so you have to look on each company page. You can also find opportunities on the University and Colleges Admission Service. Here you will find a mixture of traditional degrees and apprenticeships at various levels. Work is currently taking place to consolidate the opportunities into UCAS, but until then here are a few useful sites:

- UCAS: ucas.com
- Find An Apprenticeship: gov.uk/apply-apprenticeship
- GetMyFirstJob: getmyfirstjob.co.uk
- Rate My Apprenticeship: ratemyapprenticeship.co.uk
- NotGoingToUni: notgoingtouni.co.uk
- Top Apprenticeship Employers: topapprenticeshipemployers.co.uk

3) Create a spreadsheet

Create a spreadsheet to document your findings. Possible headings:

- Company
- URL link
- Role
- Degree awarded
- Partner university
- Entry requirements
- Date applications open

- Date applications close
- Insight events (dates)
- Submitted (use this to track applications)
- Response

4) Research

All companies will have videos about their programmes and case studies of apprentices on their website. Do research the experiences of other apprentices. Do attend insight events, so you can speak to employers and apprentices. If events are not listed on the website, do register on the site and notifications will be sent to you. Research the company's values, mission statement and behaviours.

5) LinkedIn

If you do not already have a LinkedIn account, take the time to create one. Ensure you complete your profile with a professional photo taken on your phone. Ensure you complete all of the sections of the profile, so it markets you as the best candidate. Companies often use LinkedIn for easy application submission. You can submit your profile when you find an opportunity. You can also follow companies on LinkedIn, so you receive notifications when their applications open.

6) Read reviews

In today's world of social media, there will be lots of content on YouTube, Instagram, TikTok and others, showcasing learners' journeys. You can also read reviews on RateMyApprenticeship. When you begin following companies on LinkedIn, you will also receive content about their organisation and their employees.

7) Practice makes perfect

Don't wait until you have been invited to an interview to practise your interview technique. You should always have an answer for why you make the best candidate for the role. Preparing this answer gives you insight to your skills and attributes and how you will add value to the organisation.

8) Your CV

Create your CV. If you feel the content on your CV needs additional experiences to showcase your skills use the summer to identify enrichment activities that will help boost your skills and personal development. This will ensure that you have sufficient examples and experiences when you enter the application season.

9) Attend the open days of the partner universities

As mentioned, each company will have a partner university. Attend an open day to hear more about how they deliver their part of the programme. Engage with students currently studying there and ask any questions.

10) Keep your options open

When researching degree apprenticeships, keep your options open. Review companies with a wide lens. Each company will offer a range of programmes, so explore opportunities at a variety of companies. For instance, engineering companies require business students. Each company is a business and will have finance, procurement, sales and marketing functions, so expand your search to both tech and non-tech firms.

Summary

Finding an apprenticeship can be challenging, as there is no one platform and there are no set dates when the opportunities open. During year 13, some will open in September, but others will open in March, so there is a constant need to keep searching for opportunities. With research and drive you will be able to compile a list of opportunities and be ready for the application season. It is a competitive process, but the more you prepared you are, the better you will be able to compete.

3.
PREPARING TO COMPETE

Developing the skills, behaviours and mindsets to become a degree apprentice

Applying for degree apprenticeships is competitive. Demand outstrips the supply (UCAS, 2023), so it is important that you do your research and prepare for each stage of the selection process. It is argued that one in three students (UCAS/Sutton Trust Report 2023) do not receive support with their applications, so below are the tips needed to help you prepare yourself for the selection process.

Top ten skills and behaviours

It is important to understand the key skills valued by employers. We have reviewed recent degree apprenticeship schemes and identified a list of top ten skills and behaviours valued by employers.

1) Commercial awareness

Commercial awareness is having an understanding of the challenges and opportunities faced by the industry. To become commercially aware, begin reading newspapers and industry-related articles. Reading the company's annual report will also give you an insight to the company. This can often be found on their website.

2) Embrace change

In a climate of continual change, the ability to adapt is essential. Having come through Covid, many students have learnt to adjust in different situations.

3) Critical thinking / data analysis

Critical thinking is embedded in your courses, requiring analysis of information and data in a structured approach to develop solutions to complex problems. This skill is transferable to all companies where it is a must to be innovative and develop creative solutions.

4) Ability to collaborate

The ability to work in a team, respect others' opinions and collaboratively develop a solution representative of all involved is essential in organisations today. This ability is often tested in group tasks at assessment centres. The coursework in your studies will also support the development of this skill.

5) Organisation

The ability to prioritise in view of deadlines and recognise the impact of non-completion on others is essential. Great organisational skills are needed for your studies and are directly transferable to the workplace.

6) Attitude

Having a positive attitude and a willingness to learn can be a great quality at this stage in your career. There is so much to learn that a willingness to engage and get involved can only benefit your experience.

7) Growth mindset

The willingness to keep learning new skills is integral in a degree apprenticeship and is essential in managing the impact of industry technology on how organisations operate.

8) Empathy

The ability to empathise and understand the experiences of others is a key attribute to working in a team.

9) Emotional intelligence

Having emotional intelligence allows you to gain an insight into your own emotions and those of people around you. It's a perspective that allows you to manage conflict, engage with others and empathise with them.

10) Cultural intelligence

Awareness of different cultures and customs is paramount when working in companies, where teams are from diverse backgrounds and which serve customers with different cultures, both globally and locally. An awareness of different cultures will help you connect to both teams and clients.

Extracurricular activities

Extracurricular activities help students build the skills to compete. By engaging in them, you step outside your comfort zone, which will help you build the confidence to compete in the selection processes. There are many activities in which you can engage at school, in the local community or online, although you have to find a balance between achieving grades and developing beyond the curriculum.

When applying for degree apprenticeships, you will be expected to deliver presentations, showcase your problem-solving skills, work in a team, and analyse and interpret information. You can begin building these skills by just getting involved and getting used to working with others who you may not know. If you are part of a sports team, for example, it is good preparation for attending an assessment centre with a new group of applicants.

Confidence and resilience

Confidence and resilience are essential attributes when applying for roles. It's not always going to be a yes when you apply for a role. It's the same when you play a football or netball game; your team will not always win. It's how you bounce back that counts; how you motivate your team to build the drive and determination for the next game. It's the ability to reflect and receive honest feedback about your performance and implement it. It applies to any competitive engagement, including maths challenges or business pitches. So engage in activities that stretch and challenge you, as it is in this space that you will grow.

Work experience

Understanding how business works from customer service to developing products and services will help to explore the roles you want to apply for. There are many online opportunities to gain virtual work experience or to apply for in-person events at companies, including work experience. All companies will hold insight events or visit your school to explain the range of degree apprenticeships on offer. Register on the company websites to receive updates on work experience opportunities. Other sources for work experience include Springpod, (springpod.com) which has a number of virtual work experiences for students. Explore our partner websites, Accenture, Rolls-Royce and Microsoft: all have opportunities for you to learn, grow and excel.

Be a self-starter and learn a new skill

The ability to be a self-starter and the willingness to learn something new outside your curriculum demonstrates a number of skills. Companies will value such drive and determination as they are operating in an environment that is continually changing. It does not have to be technical. It could be a new language. Or organising a fundraiser for a local cause by learning how to bake cakes is an excellent example. The skill you choose can match your personal goals and what time you have available.

Volunteering

Volunteering is a great way to develop your skills, as well as supporting a good cause. The wonderful thing about volunteering is that you can do it for an hour a day during your school holidays. It can fit around your timetable. Volunteering is filled with personal development opportunities ranging from building communication skills, developing customer service skills, working in a charity shop, event planning to building a website. The possibilities are endless. Find a cause you are passionate about and offer to volunteer.

Positions of responsibility

Being a prefect or caring for a younger sibling is a great way to showcase many valuable skills. As a prefect, you will liaise between students and teachers, which is a role that relies on communicating well and being personable. Communication, patience and attention to detail are required when looking after a younger sibling, especially if you are collecting them from school, taking them home and keeping them safe. These are great examples for your application form. Tutoring or being a buddy to another student at school is another opportunity to demonstrate your ability to communicate.

4.
YOUR CV

Summarise your achievements in six sections on your curriculum vitae

Your CV is a culmination of your work experience, school projects, extracurricular activities and your education. Some employers will ask you to complete their application form, but others will ask you to complete a CV. Your CV should be no more than two sides of A4. A CV should have a number of key sections:

- Personal details
- Profile
- Education/schools
- Qualifications

- Achievements
- Work experience / school projects
- Volunteering/responsibilities
- Hobbies

Section 1: personal details

- **Name**: state your first name and last name at the top of the page. Use a slightly bigger font and make it bold. For example: Anthony Cheval.

- **Email**: ensure you include your contact details so the employer can contact you. There's no need for your home address as the employer will email you or phone you. Your email address should just be your user name at your provider. Develop a professional email address and ensure you check your email daily. Remember to look in the spam folder. You do not want to miss an opportunity because you didn't check your email.

- **Mobile**: include your mobile number with any country codes. A UK mobile would read +44 7956 123123. Do double check the number. Triple check your mobile is correct.

Section 2: profile

To be or not to be? There are those that argue that the CV does not need a profile piece, but others, who argue that profiles provide a summary of your skills, attributes and values. As a sixth form student with limited work experience, it is important to capture how you can add value to the organisation. Your profile is a summary of your personal brand; it's an introduction to you. Students often find it hard to write a summary. Try to reflect on what makes you, you; what makes you stand out. Understanding your unique skills and traits will help you to write your profile. Avoid generic terms like 'hardworking' or 'good communicator'.

A starting point is to review the job description. How do your skills relate to the skills highlighted in the job description: how can you add value to the organisation? By reviewing the skills and attributes that the job is looking for, it will help you to highlight and relate your skills back to the role.

For example, if the role asks for a growth mindset, this means they want a student who is willing to continually learn new skills. Identify, where you have developed an extra skill in or outside of the classroom. In your profile you might state you are an independent learner or excited to learn new skills.

Here's a checklist for writing your profile:

- Length: no more than three to six sentences.
- Showcase your skills and how they align with the role. Reread the job description to ensure you know what skills and attributes are needed.
- Outline why you are the right candidate for the role.

Section 3: education

List your schools chronologically (in date order) with the most recent first. State the qualifications you gained. If you are awaiting results, include predicted grades and state awaiting results. As an example, see figure 1.

Langdon Park High School 2014–21

QUALIFICATIONS: A-LEVELS 2021

| Mathematics | A | Computer science | C | Economics | B |

QUALIFICATIONS: GCSE GRADES 2019

Mathematics	8	English literature	7	Chemistry	C
English language	6	Religious studies	C	Biology	A
Physics	7	Computer science	8	Business studies	A

Figure 1: example of how to list schools and qualifications

Section 4: achievements

Highlight achievements from any of your extracurricular activities including sports, the Duke of Edinburgh Award, debate club etc. All your extracurricular activities will help you to develop valuable skills that can help you demonstrate why you are suitable for a role. State if you are a prefect or have another role within the school. All these roles help you to build transferable skills. Provide a summary of any short courses you have completed. These can include first aid, coding courses or languages.

Section 5: work experience or school projects

List all your work experience in chronological order with the most recent first. If you have not completed any work experience, you can include any volunteering or projects that you might have completed as part of your coursework. Review your commitments at home, do you complete any tasks that you could showcase on your CV? For example, tutoring younger siblings, babysitting or collecting siblings from school all demonstrate a level of responsibility and trustworthiness that any organisation would value.

Describe the role, providing a brief description including your responsibilities. Outline the impact of your contribution. When writing the summary of your work experience, highlight the following elements:

- **Achieved**: what did you achieve? Review the results following your contribution.
- **Developed**: what skills did you develop?
- **Lead**: did you lead on the project? how did you manage the team?
- **Customer experience**: how did you contribute to the customer experience?
- **Contributed**: how did you support an event, a process or a group project?
- **Delivered**: have you delivered a talk or presentation? what was the focus? who did you deliver the talk to? what was the feedback?

Work experience / volunteering / school roles

Example 1

State the organisation: St Johns Summer Camp, Summer 2019.
State your role title: camp mentor to children aged 9–15.

- Organised and supervised activities and aided children with any challenges.
- Attended safeguarding training to ensure the safety of camp members.
- Achieved positive feedback stating that the children rated their camp experience as 9/10.

Example 2

Langdon Park High, reading buddy scheme, September 2021–present

- Supported year 7 students with their reading.
- Listened to them read and helped them to increase their confidence in reading.
- Encouraged them to ask questions and to attempt difficult words.

- Recorded new words and created a game to test them on the new words in the next session.

Example 3

Maths tutor, summer 2020–present

- Taught keystage 2 maths to my sibling.
- Developed exercises and tests to support learning and understanding.
- Created games to make the learning fun and to maintain her concentration.
- Increased her exam scores and her love of maths.

Example 4

Basketball team fundraising committee

- Developed activities and events to raise funds for new team kit.
- Created marketing materials to promote the funday.
- Supported a sports funday for junior members and raised £250.

Figure 2: examples of work experience / volunteering / school roles

Section 6: hobbies

Finally, always list your hobbies and interests as these can be great icebreakers, when you share the same interests as your interviewer. Your interests do not always need to be in line with the role, as it demonstrates a wider range of interests.

5.
INTERVIEWS AND ASSESSMENTS

After your application is accepted, your next challenge is to present yourself as well as you can at interviews and assessment centres

If you are successful through the first stage of the application process, then you will be invited to an interview. The interview may take place virtually or face to face but either way there's a range of things that you can do to help be prepared for the questions that might be asked.

Research

Research the company prior to the interview. Your search should highlight the following:

- The company mission statement and values.
- New developments or investment areas.
- Current challenges and how they are developing solutions.
- Company case studies on their website.
- Any candidate information about their selection processes.

Where can you find this information:

- On the company website.
- Newspapers articles.
- The company annual report.
- Videos on YouTube.
- The company social media accounts, including Instagram and LinkedIn.

This will help you to shape your answers for the interview and give you a good insight to how your skills and interests match to the company.

Use the STARR Method

Storytelling is a great skill to have to relay your experiences to the interviewer. All too often during an interview, when responding to a question, you can lose track. The STARR method helps you to structure your responses. Use this method to ensure that you answer the question. STARR stands for the five stages of your reply.

- **Situation**: provide the context within which you developed the skill. This could be a project at school, work experience or a volunteering position. Roles of responsibility at home can also be used, such as tutoring a younger sibling or collecting younger siblings from school.

- **Task**: outline the task that was completed, including a summary of the task and any deadlines provided. Identify any challenges to be overcome.

- **Actions**: what actions were used to complete the task, any specific skills you utilised. Describe your role and what actions you took. Avoid speaking about the overall team, as the interview is about what you specifically did.

- **Result**: provide an outcome for the task. The task does not always have to be successful; the focus is more on the actions you took. Interviewers are interested in the decisions you made, how you managed/interacted with others. Is there anything you would do differently?
- **Reflect**: reflect on the outcome. Did the results meet the requirements of the project? If you had to do it again, what would you do differently.

By using this framework your answers become structured and concise. More importantly when you are nervous, it helps you to not lose track of your points.

Preparing for the video interview

A video interview can take a number of formats:

- An interviewer on a call with you.
- A prerecording stating the questions or scenario.
- The questions just appear on the screen.

Regardless of the situation, ensure you have prepared the following:

- **Quiet space**: find a quiet space to conduct the interview. If you lack space at home speak to your school about organising a space.

- **Consistent Wifi**: to avoid disruption during your interview ensure you have access to a stable WiFi connection. The interviews often give you between three and five days to complete it, so there is time to speak with your teachers and arrange a room at school.

- **Dress code**: dress code can vary across industries, but a shirt and a jacket or a blouse are staple pieces for interviews. If you are applying for more creative industries, you can be more creative with your appearance, but for traditional industries like banking or law a shirt tie and suit are more acceptable. Your school uniform is also a good option.

- **How to practise for a video interview:** to practise for a video interview, use your phone to record yourself answering interview questions. This is a great way to review how you express yourself on the call. It enables you to review your answers, your mannerisms, your environment. Is your answer clear? Watch videos on the company website to help understand what they are looking for in new recruits.

What type of questions will they ask?

Competency-based questions

Competency-based questions focus on your ability to demonstrate how you have used a specific skill. Examples include:

- Give an example when you have worked in a team.
- Tell us a time when you had to resolve a conflict.
- Tell us about your biggest achievement to date.
- Tell us about a time when you had to resolve a problem.

Strength-based questions

Strength-based interviews allow the natural skills and ability of the candidates to shine. The interviewer gains a better understanding of the candidate's personality, their likes and dislikes, giving them a better perspective of their fit for the role. Candidates are asked to draw on their personal experiences and hobbies. Interviewers use the skills required for the role to devise questions to showcase how your strengths will be suitable. By matching your strengths to the role, it should lead to not only a better fit, but also a role that the candidate will excel in. Examples include:

- What do you excel in?
- What were your favourite subjects at school and why?
- What motivates you in life?
- What are your areas for development?
- Why do you think you are suited to this role?
- Describe an achievement you are proud of and why.

Situational-judgment questions

Situational-judgment questions are based upon scenarios you will experience in the role/workplace. The questions try to gauge the candidates' responses and see if they are in line with the company's values, ways of working and overall culture. It is important to be yourself, but also to understand the role, the company and its culture and beliefs. Situational-judgment tests can be delivered as an online test in a multiple-choice format or as questions in an interview.

Example 1

You have been asked to make a presentation to a client on a new technology to help them make a process more efficient. The presentation is scheduled for five days and whilst you have a general understanding of the technology, you do not think you have a deep enough understanding to give the presentation. What should you do? Rank best to worse.

A) Ask your manager for a more experienced colleague to deliver the presentation, as you know they have the knowledge required to deliver it flawlessly, but advise you will help prepare and, if allowed, present the presentation

B) Ask another team member, who is willing to do the presentation, and offer this person to your manager as a replacement for you, as you do not feel comfortable doing it.

C) Research deeper into the technology and ask those with experience of using it for their understanding of it, so you can incorporate this into the presentation. Also ask a more experienced colleague if they wouldn't mind sparing some time to do a practice run, so they can highlight any areas you might have missed out.

D) Try to give the presentation with the knowledge you have and hope it is enough to satisfy the clients.

Example 2

You have just joined an apprenticeship programme and have been tasked with an action you have not done before or have no knowledge of what should be done. What should you do? Rank from best to worse.

A) Tell your manager you have not done this before: could you be shown how?

B) Tell your manager, you have not done this, can someone else more experienced to do it, as you are new and do not want to complete the task wrong.

C) Ask a colleague who has experience with this task, for some help and guidance

D) Try to make a go at it alone, if stuck, then ask a colleague who has knowledge of the task for some help

E) Try to complete the task independently, not sure if you are doing it correctly, and wait for feedback after submission to see if it was right.

Assessment centres

Often the final stage of the selection process is through an assessment centre (AC). These can vary in form depending on the company, but generally consist of an interview, presentation, group task and possibly an individual task in the form of a case study. The AC can take place online or in person.

The presentation

The company can set a presentation topic prior to the AC or during the assessment you will be given a challenge and asked to prepare a presentation. The key to the presentation is to keep it simple. Avoid trying to cover everything and identify what the top three or four points are for making your case. Here's a common way that you could structure your presentation:

- Define the problem.

- Outline data as evidence of the problem.

- Outline your solution.

- Explain how your solution addresses the problem (whether as cost savings, process efficiency, better sustainability or more availability).

- Indicate the cost to implement your solution.

- Outline any limitations.

Group tasks

During the group tasks, you will be part of a team responding to a challenge presented by the company. When in the AC, remember:

- The exercise is timed, so manage your time, ie, divide your time across brainstorming, planning and summarising your ideas.

- Share your thoughts: you are being assessed, so do speak, engage and collaborate.

- Analyse other members' ideas, build on them, ask questions. Know your thoughts and ideas are just as valuable.

- Avoid speaking over others, find a space to share your ideas.

- Invite quieter members into the conversation.

- Being successful in an assessment centre is not always the person who speaks the most: it is the person who really demonstrates the ability to work in a team and collaborate with others.

- Ensure you are respectful of all your team members' ideas.

- Candidates will be reviewed in line with the values and behaviours of the company.

PART 2

EMPLOYER PROFILES

6.
DEGREE APPRENTICESHIPS WITH ACCENTURE

Profile of what one of the world's leading strategy and technology consultants offers its degree apprentices

Accenture is a leading global professional services company that helps the world's leading businesses, governments and other organisations build their digital core, optimise their operations, accelerate revenue growth and enhance citizen services, creating tangible value at speed and scale. We are a talent- and innovation-led company with approximately 743,000 people serving clients in more than 120 countries. Technology is at the core of change today, and we are one of the world's leaders in helping drive that change, with strong ecosystem relationships. We combine our strength in technology and leadership in cloud, data and artificial intelligence with unmatched industry experience, functional expertise and global delivery capability. We are uniquely able to deliver tangible outcomes because of our broad range of services, solutions and assets across strategy and consulting, technology, operations, industry X and Song. These capabilities, together with our culture of shared success and commitment to creating 360° value, enable us to help our clients reinvent and build trusted, lasting relationships. We measure our success by the 360° value we create for our clients, each other, our shareholders, partners and communities. Visit us at accenture.com.

What makes your organisation stand out?

Our values shape our culture and define our character. We live our core values through individual behaviours that guide how we act and make decisions. Our core values are:

- Client value creation
- One global network
- Respect for the individual
- Best people
- Integrity
- Stewardship

We believe a shared ethical culture is critical to our growth in a competitive marketplace. Our clear corporate-governance structure and our ethics-and-compliance programme, grounded in our core values and code of business ethics, guide our strategic business decisions and actions as we strive to foster a culture of integrity, transparency, inclusivity and respect for all people. Accenture has been recognised on Ethisphere's 2022 list of the world's most ethical companies, our 15th consecutive year on the list, and a testament to our dedication to ethical leadership, compliance practices and sustainability. Find out more in our report, *360° Value* (at accenture.com).

What role do apprentices play in your talent strategy?

The aim of Accenture's apprenticeship programme is to expand our talent pool by finding, training and developing bright young people who are keen to pursue a career in technology or consulting with Accenture. This is part of our broader commitment to creating entry-level opportunities across these sectors, where there is a skills shortage.

By tackling this skills gap, we want to help ensure that young people can develop the specialised skills needed to thrive in the digital economy. We have developed a strategic, pro-active engagement programme which is designed to meet Accenture's current and future workforce demands. We believe that a diverse workforce that reflects the clients and communities we serve is crucial to success. The apprenticeship programme is a core part of our strategy to boost diversity. Focusing on gender, ethnicity and social mobility, we continuously work with schools, colleges and third-sector organisations to create our future workforce, promoting and signposting young people to our employment opportunities at all levels.

What programmes do you have? and how are they delivered?

We offer two main apprenticeship programmes: a technology degree apprenticeship and a consulting degree apprenticeship. Visit accenture.com/ukapprentices to find out more.

Technology degree apprenticeship

What does it involve?

- Technology is the future of the world and on this programme you will work with some of the most innovative technologies to transform the businesses of our clients. You will work across a range of industries to improve efficiencies and develop multiple capabilities, including digital, web, data, cloud computing, application project management and infrastructure development.

- Apprentices receive an average of six hours' off-the-job training a week. You'll usually have one day at university and four days a week at Accenture. Our apprenticeships include a combination of block and day release. This involves two weeks of block release and one day at university, dependent on location.

What qualification will I receive once I've completed the degree?

- BSc Degree in digital and technology solutions with various specialisms depending on location.

Do I need technology or technical experience to apply for this programme?

- No. If you are interested and passionate about the future of technology, you are the perfect candidate. We do not require any prior experience or expect you to have studied specific subjects. You will undertake comprehensive training on joining, which will be supplemented at university and on client site. At Accenture, we ensure that you are equipped with the relevant knowledge and skills to effectively kickstart your career in technology.

Who's eligible?

- You should have the right to work and study a degree in the UK.

- For London, you will need 80 UCAS points based on A-level qualifications or other equivalent level-3 qualifications. Other locations may vary. Please review our website for further information.

What's the duration of the programme?

- The duration of our programme is three years, although it may vary by location.

- Once you complete the apprenticeship, you will graduate with your bachelor's degree and be promoted into an analyst position within the company,.

Consulting degree apprenticeship

What does it involve?

- Consulting is very people focused. You'll work as part of a project team to build enduring, trust-based relationships at the heart of a client's organisation, helping them to address their most significant business issues. This will be focused on specific industries: financial services; products; communications, media and technology; health & public services; and resources. You'll develop expertise across a range of capabilities, including business economics, strategic management, business operations, business accounting, researching business data and many more.

- You will attend the University of East London once a week and work for the remaining four days with our clients.

What's the qualification I will receive once I've completed the degree?

- BSc (Hons) Practitioner in organisational management and leadership with a chartered manager status.

What's the duration of the programme?

- The duration of our programme is three years. Once you have completed the apprenticeship, you will graduate with your bachelor's degree (Hons) and be looking to be promoted into a higher position within the company.

Who's eligible?

- You should have the right to work and study at degree level in the UK.
- Five GCSEs (A-C or 4-9) including maths and English.
- You will need 80 UCAS points across A-levels or other equivalent level-3 qualifications.

Support for apprentices

- **Sub-community leads:** interlock with university, apprentices and apprenticeship manager, ensuring that apprentices have the relevant support to succeed.
- **People lead:** helps the apprentices navigate their careers at Accenture, including assisting with targets, priorities and reviewing progress for talent discussions.
- **Line manager:** direct report, responsible for aligning tasks to apprentices and setting key objectives across projects.
- **Buddy:** current apprentice with at least six months' experience. Key contact for apprentices throughout the programme, providing helpful hints and tips based on past experience.

- **Apprenticeship manager**: main liaison with the university, ensuring that the apprentices are provided with quality training and the relevant support. Responsible for overall programme management.

- **HR partner**: responsible for staffing apprentices on projects that align with career aspirations and university priorities. Provides guidance on key organisational processes and procedures.

- **Course lead:** your course leader who will be able to guide you regarding any university enquiries or issues.

Benefits to apprentices

- No debt but you will still have the opportunity to gain a degree.
- Large starting community/cohort, enabling apprentices to form strong networks.
- Experience at a reputable firm.
- Access to networks, for example, mental health allies, African and Caribbean network, sports clubs and interest groups like rugby, football and yoga.

- Client and project experiences across a variety of industries.
- Volunteering days to support causes you are passionate about.
- Working with top experts in industries.

What does diversity and social mobility mean to your organisation?

We are committed to accelerating equality for all and to creating a work environment where all of our people feel like they belong. We have an unwavering commitment to diversity. Each of our people should have a full sense of belonging within our organisation. As a business imperative, every person at Accenture has the responsibility to create and sustain an inclusive environment for all.

Inclusion and diversity are fundamental to our culture and core values. Our rich diversity makes us more innovative and more creative, which helps us better serve our clients and our communities.

We are building a culture of equality, based on respect, inclusiveness and shared ethical values, to ensure our people can achieve their professional and personal aspirations.

We recognise that true belonging means being accepted for who we are. To enable our people to present their authentic selves, we take a zero-tolerance stance on discrimination based on ethnicity, gender, sexual orientation, disability or any other form of diversity.

Diversity of thought and lived experiences are crucial to unlocking new value. Different perspectives create new thinking and new solutions, enabling us to better serve our clients and communities. As we lead through change, we continue to go beyond compliance, building trust into everything we do, exercising good judgement and always acting with integrity.

Being a degree apprentice: comment by Teyah Davis

A day in the life

Honestly, my days can really vary. Overall, I can say with certainty that it all blends into the best thing that ever happened to me.

At university, days are pretty normal: a mixture of lectures and labs with the rest of my cohort, working on content in alignment with our BSc in digital and technology solutions.

At work, I'll usually start by logging on and checking my emails. I like to have a clear inbox, so I know exactly what I've got to do. I'll usually then join my stand-up call with my team, which involves everyone talking about what they worked on yesterday, what they plan to work on today and anything preventing them from making progress. There's always a sprinkle of conversation about the weather because my teams are always based all around the world. I've done stand-ups with people in Austria, Germany, Spain and even as far away as India.

Once I've gotten to the end of that, I make a start on my actual tasks. I'm a backend software developer. I primarily work with JavaScript and AWS, so on a practical level, I pick up tickets from our team backlog, and start writing some code, fighting some bugs, writing technical documentation or supporting team members with their tasks.

I've experienced loads of different roles, including blockchain engineer, tester, business analyst and dev-ops engineer to name a few.

My favourite part about this scheme is the freedom I have to get involved with the wider organisation. Since joining, I've been given the opportunity to singlehandedly design and lead programmes in schools and colleges across London for students from low socioeconomic backgrounds and I've been able to have a greater impact than I could've ever imagined.

Why did you choose the degree apprenticeship as opposed to going to university?

I knew university would bore me. I've always been a hands-on learner and I wanted to get as involved as I possibly could from as early on as possible. University just wasn't right for me for this reason. Also, I quickly figured, by going to multiple insight days and various employers, that most computer-science graduates were coming out of university with a lot of theory and very little industry experience. I didn't want to be in a situation where after completing an intense degree, I would have to compete in a tough graduate market over jobs that I wasn't guaranteed to enjoy, so a degree apprenticeship made the most sense because I knew that I would end up with three years of industry experience and a guaranteed job at the end.

Additionally, I like money. I wanted to put myself in a better financial position than the one I was in and all I associated university with was crippling debt that never gets paid off. Though that's a bit of an exaggeration, I preferred the idea of earning whilst learning in a relevant field to working an irrelevant part-time job whilst trying to keep up with assignments.

Though I faced discouragement from a bunch of different places, like school for example, where they tried to get me to write a UCAS personal statement just in case, I knew what I wanted and I knew that I couldn't get that from university.

Finally, in terms of my professional network, I knew that a degree apprenticeship would give me the foundation I needed to learn as much as I possibly could. Learning from peers is valuable, but working alongside some of the best minds all over the world was the winning decision.

How do you balance studying while working?

Starting everything immediately. I didn't stick to this for the whole three years of my degree, but for the most part, if I got a task, an assignment, a piece of work, I would start on it immediately.

Leaving things to the last minute is always a big stressor for me. I knew that my full-time job had deadlines, which were significantly more important because they involved live systems and services for clients all over the world, I knew that if I wanted to minimise my stress, I would have to eliminate all my little tasks as quickly as possible.

During the busiest periods, my week would look like going to university on Monday, then working Tuesday to Friday for my normal hours, logging off and immediately logging on to complete my university work. I gave myself a break on Saturdays, then Sundays were university days again.

What advice would you give to a student thinking about a degree apprenticeship?

Do your research. Figure out if it's actually the right path for you. Learn as much as you possibly can, whether from the internet, friends, family, current apprentices, company insight events. Put the work in to figure out if it's what you genuinely want, because as much as you go through their interview processes, they need to go through yours.

Stop being scared. There's so much you won't understand. You won't know about the companies, the jobs and the industries, but it doesn't matter. We all start from somewhere. We don't start knowing everything, so admit when you don't know something, and figure out how you can learn.

Expect what you put in. The degree apprenticeship experience is often what you make of it. So if you go into it apprehensive and reserved, you'll probably leave feeling the same way. If you go in excited to learn and prepared to make mistakes, you'll have the opportunity to learn and grow at a phenomenal pace.

Being a degree apprentice: comment by Daniel Bolarinwa

A day in the life

Contrary to common stereotypes in mass media, apprentices don't make coffee or run errands for senior team members. I'm a testament to that. I currently work as a backend engineering tech lead, holding a significant role on my project. First, let's clarify what that entails before delving into a typical day in my life.

Imagine yourself visiting a restaurant. You take a seat, look through the menu, decide on your food and drinks, and place your order through a waiter. The waiter then communicates your order to the chefs, who prepare your meal and drinks. Finally, the waiter brings your order to your table. Translating that into a technology context, when you visit websites like Amazon, you browse their catalogue, select items to purchase, and proceed to buy them. After clicking the purchase button, technology components called APIs (application programming interfaces) process your order and communicate with other systems to retrieve necessary information for delivering your order to your house. These APIs act as the waiters in this analogy.

As a backend engineering tech lead, I oversee the development of these APIs and other downstream systems that enable smooth user interactions in an application. My responsibilities include participating in daily team update meetings, researching and designing the logical flow of the systems we build, refining system requirements with senior client stakeholders, delegating tasks to team members, and personally contributing to the development of crucial components of those systems.

Apart from work, degree apprentices also engage in university, pursuing a degree chosen by their employer. This typically involves attending lectures and labs at the university for one or two days a week, dedicated to completing assignments or readings. It is important to note that the apprentice experience varies for each individual, but I hope this illustrates the impact and fulfilment it can offer.

Why did you choose a degree apprenticeship as opposed to going to university?

I once held the belief that my future would revolve around studying medicine and pursuing a career as a surgeon. However, that perception took a dramatic turn. During my time in secondary school, I accompanied some friends to a sixth form open evening where we casually visited the computer science department. Unexpectedly, this visit became the catalyst for a significant change in my aspirations.

The allure of the technology industry captivated me, particularly the ability to transform ideas into reality through programming and problem-solving skills. Nevertheless, I recognised the importance of obtaining a degree to meet my parents' expectations. Opting for a degree apprenticeship seemed like the perfect solution. It offered a pathway to enter the industry I was passionate about at an earlier stage, acquiring valuable skills while simultaneously satisfying my parents' desire for me to earn a degree.

Did I also mention the degree is debt free? This played a major factor in my decision as a degree apprenticeship was the better financial decision for me compared to accruing over £27,000 of debt at a university.

How do you balance studying while working?

The most effective way I found of balancing studying while working is to be proactive with university deadlines. It seems obvious, but it can be quite easy to overlook and implement. By completing university assignments and readings as early as possible, you gain additional time to concentrate on your work responsibilities while also receiving iterative feedback on the assignments you have submitted.

Being ahead of schedule provides ample opportunity to delve into challenging subject concepts or content, ensuring a solid foundation for exam preparations and essay submissions. Additionally, forming mini groups or friendships with fellow apprentices plays a vital role in balancing studying and work. Collaborating with others allows for knowledge sharing and mutual support. It is often the case that someone in the group complements your strengths and understands the aspects that you may find difficult and vice versa. This collaborative dynamic can greatly enhance your learning experience and overall success.

What advice would you give to a student thinking about a degree apprenticeship?

- You need to be passionate for the industry you want to move into because apprenticeships can be difficult, doing a degree while working in time-pressured environments. If you lack passion for what you apply for, you will quickly find yourself not enjoying it.

- Apply for it, take the leap of faith, the first step into the industry. There is no limit to the success you can achieve as an apprentice. Doing an apprenticeship puts you in a space that university cannot. You get to gain heavily sought-after industry skills, exposure to experienced industry professionals who are very supportive and so much more.

- Be yourself. There is no playbook or guidelines of how to operate in a workplace; you shouldn't change your personality to fit a particular mould of candidates or you'll just be another part of the herd. Being yourself will help you to stand out because no two people are built the same. Our experiences are different and so are our strengths.

Applying to Accenture

All interested candidates are able to apply via our website: accenture.com/ukapprentices. Before applying, we advise candidates to be as prepared as they can:

- Complete the Accenture x Forage work experience programme (accenture.com/gb-en/careers/local/virtual-experience-program).
- Research Accenture at accenture.com/apply.
- Read Accenture blogs (in the UK, see accenture.com/gb-en/blogs/blogs-ukcareers).

Candidates can stand out by demonstrating:

- Authenticity.
- Passion/interest for your selected area.
- Research.
- Problem-solving skills.
- Collaboration and communication skills.
- A commitment and willingness to invest in your learning and development, devoting the time to the training and study required.

Tips during the application process:

- **Digital profile (digital CV):** include all possible information, qualifications and skills to support you in the process. Review the job description and Accenture website to pull some relevant information or words that resonate with you and your profile. Ensure you answer all contextual and eligibility questionnaires.

- **Online assessment:** there are no time restrictions. Feel free to take as long as you need when tackling this challenge. Read all questions carefully and don't miss anything out. Ensure you research Accenture, such as checking out our core values.

- **Assessment centres:** attend the recruiter assessment centre sessions where you will receive some handy tips. Ensure you demonstrate your passion for Accenture, technology, openness to learning and remember to remain authentic. We want to learn more about you as an individual. Research strength-based interviews.

- **Technical interview:** whilst we are not looking for any particular technical skills, you need to demonstrate passion for technology and desire to develop a career in this area. You can demonstrate this passion through research on YouTube, LinkedIn, TikTok and discuss these during the interview. You will receive further hints and tips from your recruiter ahead of this interview.

7.
DEGREE APPRENTICESHIPS AT MICROSOFT

Profile of what to expect as a degree apprentice at one of the world's leading technology companies

Microsoft's mission is to empower every person and every organisation on the planet to achieve more. We are committed to innovation, diversity, social responsibility and customer satisfaction. Founded in 1975 by Bill Gates and Paul Allen, who wanted to create a personal computer revolution, today Microsoft is one of the most valuable and influential companies in the world, with over 220,000 employees and more than 1.3 billion customers.

Microsoft develops and sells a wide range of products and services, such as cloud computing, software, hardware, gaming and artificial intelligence. Some of the most popular Microsoft products and services are:

- **Windows**: the operating system that powers most of the world's PCs, laptops, tablets and phones. Windows is known for its user-friendly interface, security features and compatibility with various devices and applications.

- **Microsoft 365**: the suite of productivity apps that includes Word, Excel, PowerPoint, Outlook, OneNote and more. Microsoft 365 helps users create, communicate, collaborate and manage their work and personal data.

- **Azure**: the cloud computing platform that offers a range of services for building, deploying and managing applications and data on a global network of data centres. Azure supports various programming languages, frameworks, tools and databases.

- **Xbox**: the gaming console that delivers immersive gaming experiences with high-quality graphics, sound and online multiplayer features. Xbox also offers a subscription service called Xbox Game Pass that gives users access to hundreds of games for a monthly fee.

- **Bing**: the web search engine that provides fast and relevant results for queries on the internet. Bing also offers other features such as image search, video search, news search, maps, translator and more.

- **LinkedIn**: founded in 2003, LinkedIn connects the world's professionals to make them more productive and successful. With more than a billion members worldwide, including executives from every Fortune 500 company, LinkedIn is the world's largest professional network.

- **Teams**: simplify collaboration with Teams to level up your work, connect with others for greater impact and scale your business to achieve more.

- **Copilot**: AI for everything you do. Work smarter, be more productive, boost creativity and stay connected to the people and things in your life with Copilot, an AI companion that works everywhere you do and intelligently adapts to your needs.

Microsoft also supports various initiatives and programmes that aim to improve education, health care, environmental sustainability and digital inclusion around the world.

Our culture and values

Microsoft's culture and values are guiding principles that shape our vision, mission and goals. They are based on the following aspects:

- **Accountability**: we expect employees to take responsibility for their decisions, actions and results. This means being honest, ethical and trustworthy in everything they do.

- **Quality and innovation**: we strive to deliver high-quality products and services that meet or exceed customer expectations. This means being creative, curious, and willing to experiment with new ideas and technologies.

- **Responsiveness to customers**: we listen to customers and respond to their needs and feedback. This means being agile, flexible and adaptable to changing market conditions and customer preferences.

- **Growth mindset**: we encourage employees to learn from successes and failures, and seek new challenges and opportunities for personal and professional growth. This means being open-minded, collaborative and supportive of each other.

- **Diversity and inclusion**: we value the diversity of our employees and customers, fostering a culture of inclusion where everyone feels respected, valued and empowered. This means being aware of the impact of one's actions on others, and being committed to social responsibility and environmental sustainability.

These core aspects of Microsoft's culture and values define our identity and direction as a global technology leader.

What roles do apprentices play in your talent strategy?

Our mission to empower every person on the planet to achieve more can mean different things to different people, so having those people present and contributing to our solutions and culture is the only way we'll deliver technology to society that is relevant. On top of that, the statistics show that those from ethnically diverse backgrounds, as well as those from disadvantaged backgrounds, may miss out on the opportunities about which their peers are aware and naturally come across.

Therefore, being proactive and taking actions that level the playing field is the only way to make sure social mobility happens. And only then can we start to address the imbalances in representation we see.

Currently, we have three programmes in EiC: apprenticeships, internships and graduates (aspire programme). Our apprenticeship programme is unique as is it the first point of entry into Microsoft for candidates who haven't gone the traditional route (going to university and obtaining a degree). It gives potential candidates the opportunity to start their career at Microsoft without relevant work experience and a degree, and it provides them with the opportunity to gain a qualification and experience working at Microsoft. The way our programmes are delivered are through practical work experience, training and shadowing with, of course, a social element to ensure that those on the programmes are able to connect and network.

Apprentices at Microsoft: comment by Ivy Kayima, Senior Global Talent Acquisition Partner, EiC Hiring | Diversity, Equity & Inclusion

I have been working on the hiring process for the apprenticeship programme for over a year and it has been the joy of my career. I am extremely proud of the work that our team has been able to achieve, particularly in terms of the diversity of the programme.

For so many of the candidates, this is the start to a great career and the programme empowers them to grow and see that anything is possible. That is also what I believe this book will do: I am confident that it will inspire young individuals to progress towards the careers they want with practical knowledge that they can apply to their own lives.

Being truly inclusive is about bridging the gap. So many of us learn about what is out there for us when it is too late. Or at least it often feels that way. This is something we are always trying to change and raise awareness, which is why understanding how the apprenticeship route works is vital, as it may be exactly what you are looking for – and it is important to know that we are also looking for you.

Our apprentices are innovative, provide us with different perspectives and help to energise the business. They are crucial to the work we do and contribute to our success.

How do you support your apprentices?

Our apprentices can always connect with human resources, as well as their managers, to discuss how they are doing throughout their apprenticeships, be that virtually or online. They also have one-to-one meetings with their direct managers to highlight any issues they may have or any support they may need.

Why choose Microsoft for a degree apprenticeship?

One of the major benefits of undertaking a degree apprenticeship is that you will not need to pay tuition fees. At the moment, tuition fees are capped at £9250 for universities in England. This cap has remained the same since it was introduced in 2017. Since 1998, tuition fee caps have increased by 925 percent, highlighting the significance of apprenticeships. Being at Microsoft also gives you the opportunity to gain insight into other areas of the business and an understanding to how the organisation works. Also, Microsoft is one of the best technology companies in the world to work for. It's a diverse company that encourages growth, so starting your career at Microsoft on a degree apprenticeship is a great move.

Application process

There are various stages to your application:

- Apply on the website of GMFJ, Get My First Job (video application).
- If successful, you will be invited to an assessment-centre interview.
- Attend assessment-centre interview.
- Find out the outcome 48 hours after the interview.

How to prepare before applying?

- Please make sure you prepare by reading the job description to make sure that your interests align with the actual role as to start an apprenticeship is a big decision.

- You are able to pre-record your answers for the video interview via the GMFJ site, so please make sure that you don't rush your answers and make sure that you are informed.

- Go onto the Microsoft website and research our company

What makes a candidate stand out?

- If free courses are available that align with the roles you are applying for, it would be a good idea to show initiative and take them online.

Top tips and common errors at each stage?

- **Application**: please make sure your video is on when recording your answers, Show enthusiasm and motivation, display interest to the role

- **Tests**: main tip is to prepare and research the role and company.

- **Assessment centres**: it can be overwhelming to interview anywhere but always remember all the work and effort you have put in to get to this point and reassure yourself and do your best.
- **Interviews**: When interviewing we always suggest using the STARR method (ie, responding by describing the situation, the task, the action and the result).

Being a Microsoft degree apprentice: comment by Akua Apeagyei

A day in the life

Every day is different. I have a study day a week towards my university degree. The other days are either filled with shadowing, working on customer projects, developing my tech skills via taking certificate exams or building stuff on Azure portal. I am also part of the university outreach team and other ERGs, so get to organise cool workshops to help inspire and encourage others to also start their tech journey.

Why did you choose a degree apprenticeship as opposed to going to university?

The plan was to go to university but gave up on that dream due to life, but things ended up working out when I got the chance to continue to work and learn. It was like a full circle moment for me.

How do you balance studying whilst working?

With strict calendar management, which is essential for working in a corporate environment. Meeting with colleagues is a big part of accomplishing the many activities that need to be completed each day.

Being a Microsoft degree apprentice: Stephen Chege

A day in the life

Fortunately, I get to work from home, so my day in the life may not be as grand as the online videos, but it's still a different kind of experience than you may get if you were in university. Normally, the first thing I do when I start work is plan my day and the things I need to get done either for that day or sometimes for the week if I know there's a task I'll need to complete by the end of week. Once that's done, on certain days I'll have a team call. On Tuesday, I have a technology specific weekly call and on Fridays I will have an industry specific one. Team members can share ideas and discuss projects, which helps with my role as apprentice as you don't tend to be aligned to specific customers or have a constant workload like a full-time experienced employee would. Once meetings are done, I spend most of my time upskilling or working on projects for customers, such as demos, proof of concepts, workshops. Or I'm in customer meetings. By the time I've finished with all of that, my day finishes around 5:30. The only time it tends to run over is if I'm doing extra work for my university course or if I'm talking to people in other parts of the world where time zones are different. After 5:30, I'm the same as any other person having a social life and doing the things I enjoy until the next day starts at 9:00.

Why did you choose a degree apprenticeship as opposed to going to university?

I was actually ready to go university in all honesty. I saw degree apprenticeships, but never thought they were attainable. I always thought it would be a good idea to study and also make money, but I wasn't sure if I was good enough to do it. However, after meeting Frances, and participating in the EDI/Microsoft I Accelerator work experience programme, I was reassured that it was 100 percent possible. I spoke to Microsoft employees, who told me more about the culture at Microsoft and that's when I decided I'll go for it, regardless of if I get it, and here I am now. I'm enjoying every second of it both the good and the hard times. I'm also coming out with no debt from my degree and four years of industry experience.

How do you balance studying whilst working?

The way I balance it is by spending the one day a week allocated for study strictly doing it. Sometimes it may not be enough and that's where transparency with my manager comes in. I'll ask to set more time aside on a specific assignment. Most of the time, it's more than enough, if I've been able to manage my time correctly. I also use my manager and other colleagues to test my ideas about my assignments. It helps me to give me a professional viewpoint on my research. It's great being able to speak to my team, who know more than I do.

What advice would you give to a student thinking about degree apprenticeship?

Be ready to work under pressure. A degree apprenticeship is a really good way to get on to the corporate ladder, but also means you have to start living the corporate lifestyle. Managing a degree on top of a job which your manager expects you to perform won't be easy. The pressure will be a whole other experience, especially if you're coming straight out of sixth form or college. But as they say pressure makes diamonds. Be open and transparent with your manager and university skills coach. If you let them know your strengths and weaknesses, you can manage the pressure better.

Learn how to prioritise. The easiest way to feel as little pressure as possible is to learn how to manage your time to make sure you finish everything each day and each week. Time boxing and setting to-do lists for yourself helps you cope, as well as figure out what's actually important and what will help you grow to become a better person and employee. Just remember the more valuable you are for a company, the more they'll want to keep you afterwards, so learn from early to do things that matter.

Don't be scared. Many apprentices experience imposter syndrome. I do too. But what you must realise is that majority of the employees in every company also feel like they don't know enough regardless of the many years of experience they may have. So be happy to make mistakes and ask questions, because it helps you grow and learn things that will make you a much better person. What most companies look for, especially when hiring apprentices, is how well you can learn. They don't expect you to be a genius. They want someone who will push themselves out of their comfort zone to improve and understand more. So don't be scared and just jump right in there. Experienced individuals love to help out when they have the time regardless of how scary they look.

Being a Microsoft degree apprentice: Isaac Amosu

A day in the life

At Microsoft, it feels like no two days are ever the same. My day could range from delivering a full day of technical presentations and demos to my customers, coaching at hackathons, upskilling in training to general admin and having time to network with my peers and team. It truly helps to keep each and every day fresh and exciting with different ways or methods of tackling the tasks at hand, which just helps keep me engaged and drive the enjoyment from my work. Each day presents a new challenge and a new way to solve that challenge that forces you to grow as an individual and I'm personally very invested in my self-development journey.

Why did you choose a degree apprenticeship as opposed to going to university?

I chose the degree apprenticeship route due to my preferred way of learning. The ability to combine both the theoretical knowledge and the practical experience of the technology subjects you encounter in your university modules help cement what you learn as opposed to reading everything from the textbook. The advantages the degree apprentices have compared to their university counterparts cannot be ignored: university fees are not a problem, you leave with three to four years' experience and the possibility to be hired either as a full-time employee for your organisation or, depending on your field, you can always look at other organisations.

How do you balance studying whilst working?

Understand and use a system that works best for you. Understand your behaviours and motivators: what are the times you usually check? when are you most engaged and play to those behaviours? A good example is that I like to learn in the morning as that is when I have the most energy. The key is being strict and disciplined with your time, understanding your priorities as a degree apprentice, since your passing depends on you succeeding in the studying element, as well as performance in your day role.

What advice would you give to a student thinking about degree apprenticeship?

Be adaptable but be your authentic self: don't lose what makes you by trying to fit into the crowd too much. Learn from your peers and understand your environment, then apply those to yourself without losing the essence of you.

Don't use mates of your age as the stick to measure yourself by. You're going on a different journey to those going to university, so, of course, you're going to have a lot of differences with the results and milestones in your journey. Stay focused on your path and understand what good looks like for where you are going and the journey you've started.

Get a mentor. Find someone who you can trust to guide you in different elements, whether it's subject matter, balancing your work life or as general mentors.

As a degree apprentice who has graduated, what has been your experience since then?

It has been amazing. Seeing the growth within myself from where I first started to becoming a full-time employee within Microsoft has really opened my eyes to the potential I have as an individual.. The role also comes with more responsibilities and a new way of looking at things: you would have built the discipline, you would have built structure for yourself, you would have built experience in your subject matter. Now it's about driving your career the way you want to and showing all those years of growth every day.

8.
DEGREE APPRENTICESHIPS AT ROLLS-ROYCE

Profile of what one of the world's leading engineers offers its degree apprentices and how you could become one

At Rolls-Royce, our purpose is to connect, power and protect our world. Our goal is to make power safer, cleaner and more sustainable. And none of that is possible without our people.

We develop and deliver complex, safety-critical power and propulsion solutions in the air, at sea and on land. Our global company is made up of three main businesses: civil aerospace, defence and power systems.

We're an iconic brand, which might make you first think of the motor car company where we started, but we haven't made cars for over 40 years. Instead, we've designed the world's most efficient large aeroengine, powered naval nuclear submarines and achieved world records for electric flight. We've created game-changing engineering solutions for supersonic jets and even supported NASA missions on the edge of space.

Our culture and values

Everyone should feel comfortable at work and be able to be their best. For us, that means creating an environment where everybody is treated with dignity and respect.

Join us and we'll welcome you into an inclusive culture, focused on safety for our people and our products. We'll invest in you, making sure you can learn and develop the way you need to, giving you challenging and rewarding opportunities to make a difference and progress in your career.

We offer flexible working options where possible and give ample reward and recognition. Our award-winning learning platform, Leatro, helps you to build skills in any area you want to, and our focus on creating a more environmentally, socially and ethically sustainable business gives us all a rewarding purpose every day.

Our STEM (science, technology, engineering and maths) outreach activities give you the chance to share your experiences with the next generation of apprentices and our global inclusion network is an important part of our culture, connecting and celebrating people with shared characteristics or experience, such as the African and Caribbean Professional Network (ACPN); Multi-Faith Network (MFN); OPEN, for individuals with disabilities, neurodiversity or underlying health conditions; and Prism for our LGBT+ employees and their allies.

We want our people to be healthy and happy. Wellbeing is about feeling good and functioning well, so when you join our global workforce, we'll make sure you get all the support you need to maintain your physical, mental and financial wellbeing.

We take our impact seriously: from working to make power cleaner and safe to helping our people make proactive daily choices that respect our planet and reflect our values. To do this we think about everything that makes us Rolls-Royce: from what products we choose to make and how we make them, how we run our factories and our supply chains, how we treat our people, and how we all behave.

Our values are at the heart everything we do, and we actively live our values through how we behave. We commit to embrace agility, be bold and pursue collaboration. And we always seek simplicity.

Diversity and social mobility at Rolls-Royce: comment by Ellie Long, Head of Early Career Delivery

Across the whole of Rolls-Royce, we're committed to championing individuality and inclusion to create a working environment where everyone belongs and can be at their best. We know how important a diverse business is for our success. Inclusive teams, which are diverse in both make-up and thought, are better for people and better for business. In short, diversity brings different perspectives and inclusion drives performance. As we look ahead to how we'll connect, power and protect society, we need our people to be at their best; no matter who they are or what part they play in our success.

We're passionate about making sure our opportunities are accessible to all and that no one is ever disadvantaged in applying to our roles because of their background or life experience. We know we can always do better, but we're working hard to make sure that anyone leaving school and considering their options, sees a Rolls-Royce apprenticeship as a viable – and excellent – choice for their future. And that they can see that we're a business with a culture where anyone can thrive.

What role do apprentices play in your talent strategy?

The success of Rolls-Royce relies on a continuous pipeline of exceptional talent. That's why, for more than a hundred years, apprentices have been a key part of our workforce. And they're more important than ever. As advancing technologies and climate change reshape the work we do, apprenticeships are vital in developing the future skills we need. And ensuring apprentices reflect the full diversity of our society means we'll be in an even stronger position to meet the planet's power needs sustainably.

Our multimillion pound learning and development centre in Derby demonstrates our ongoing commitment to apprenticeships in particular. And today, we run no fewer than 23 separate apprenticeship schemes, across nine sites in the United Kingdom.

Our apprenticeships span the breadth of engineering and business. All offer the chance to gain practical experience, in-depth training and professional qualifications, while earning a salary.

If you're studying for, or have completed, A-levels or an equivalent qualification, we've got a wide range of higher and degree apprenticeships.

- In engineering and technology, our apprenticeships include engineering, electrical and electronics, software, materials engineering, nuclear engineering, non-destructive testing and manufacturing engineering.
- Across business and enterprise, we have apprenticeships that include business management, commercial and procurement, digital and technology solutions, finance, project management, and supply chain management.

Whichever programme you join, you'll be working on live projects while working towards debt-free qualifications. You'll get classroom training as well as on-the-job experience, working alongside technical or business experts.

How do you support your apprentices?

At Rolls-Royce, we consider the on-the-job aspect of our training to be every bit as important as the classroom learning and formal qualifications. So, our apprentices get involved with live projects, make a meaningful impact and assume real responsibility from an early stage.

The apprentice development leader assigned to you will support your individual learning plan. Managers and colleagues in the business will mentor you throughout your apprenticeship. The Apprentice and Graduate Association runs numerous social events and activities where you can mix with your peers. In our inclusion network groups, like the ACPPCN (African Caribbean Professional Network) or Prism for LGBTQ+ employees, you can meet people who share similar characteristics or life experiences to your own.

Why choose Rolls-Royce for a degree apprenticeship?

We're doing more than ever to include, develop, reward and engage our people in an environment where you can be yourself and always be your best. Here's some of the benefits of undertaking a higher or degree apprenticeship at Rolls-Royce:

- On the job experience with expert teams, working on real-life projects and cutting-edge products.

- Learning in our dedicated Apprentice Academy or Nuclear Skills Academy in Derby and/or with excellent training providers like Derby University, UAE and the University of Sheffield's Advanced Manufacturing Research Centre getting a high-quality education and qualification.

- Fully funded degree – no university debt.

- Career support from day one: excellent development, mentoring and support from business leaders and our apprenticeship team.

- A competitive salary with annual pay rises and company benefits from health and life insurance to gym discounts and cheap cinema tickets.

- Competitive pension and 33 days' holiday per year (including bank holidays).

- Your health and wellbeing are important to us: from providing healthy food in our sites and sports clubs, to our employee assistance programme, and mental health champion networks to support you wherever you need it, with whatever you are struggling with.

- Get social with your peers: get involved in our Apprentice and Graduate Association, who run social events, fundraising and leisure activities, and networking opportunities.

- Experience our inclusive and welcoming culture, be a part of our global inclusion network.

Application process

We have three stages to our application process:

- Online application form: direct to us via careers.rolls-royce.com.
- Online tests.
- Assessment centre (generally virtual): you'll be invited to an assessment centre if you are successful in the previous stages.

First start by thinking about what excites you, says Ellie Long, global early career lead. 'What gets you out of bed in the morning and what do you want to be part of? We spend most of our life at work and so you've got to do something you enjoy. You don't want to be going into an environment where you've got to mask who you are because, trust me, it gets exhausting. You've got to be in a place where you're going to be happy. So really figure out what that looks like first.'

Who is your ideal Rolls-Royce candidate?

We are often asked this question. The answer is simple. We

don't have a standard Rolls-Royce apprentice. We look for students from all backgrounds who have the motivation to want to be part of our organisation. What makes a candidate stand out is somebody who shows an interest and passion in wanting to work for us, and who demonstrates our behaviours.

Application

We don't ask for a CV, as we know a lot of students don't have these and we want to give everybody the opportunity to tell us about themselves. We'll ask you three or four questions in the online application that will include the things you're interested in and what inspires you. Don't try and tell us what you think we want to hear, show us your personality, and tell us what makes you, you. If you love to bake, can speak a different language, or you've taught yourself how to knit, these are all valuable skills. Just because we are an engineering and technology company doesn't mean we're not interested in them: we don't have 'an ideal candidate'. You might not have direct work experience or a part-time job, but you do help care for your siblings or do the shopping for an elderly neighbour. These are all life experiences that make you unique so tell us about them.

Online tests

Just do your best and don't be tempted to get somebody to help you or do the tests for you. We want to see who you are and learn more about your style of working. Find a quiet place, get yourself a drink (and maybe a snack) and try and relax. The more you overthink your responses or try and second guess the tests, the less likely you are to show your strengths. There are typically three tests and it takes about 45 minutes to complete them all. Only one of our tests is timed so you have the chance to work through the others at your own pace:

- a situational judgment exercise (SJE), which assesses decision-making (untimed);

- a logical reasoning assessment, which assesses complex problem-solving capabilities (six minutes);

- a personality assessment, which assesses your preferred ways of behaving and working (untimed).

Our top tip is to take your time, read the questions carefully and be your authentic self.

Assessment centres

Research Rolls-Royce to gain an insight into our business and have a clear understanding of why you have applied to work here. Think about what you want us to know about you, and how you can best share that with us. Identify some examples of when you have been at your best and use the STARR method to communicate them. The interviews are an opportunity to understand more about the role, what type of career progression is available and more about the function or business the role is related to. They are a discussion and your opportunity to work out whether Rolls-Royce aligns to your own values and preferences. Remember, no question is a silly question.

Stella Moseley, Rolls-Royce campus recruiter, recommends checking out the careers website and Instagram (rolls-royce_careers) which contains information and videos on the application process, and reassures applicants: 'if you have any questions or need support during or before your application, just get in touch'. She also reminds applicants that:

- At any time during the application process, Rolls-Royce will consider specific adjustments if they are needed, for example, extra time during the online assessments or other requirements for the assessment day.

- Online drop-in sessions are available before the assessment day to discuss the assessment process.
- Telephone calls follow all offers being made to give successful candidates a chance to discuss any requirements or concerns and make their first step to joining Rolls-Royce.

Being a degree apprentice: comment by Farah Saeed

A day in the life

In my current placement I have days where I can work from home and office days. If it's an office day I start my day with my two-hour commute to work. Once I arrive at the office and log in, I catch up on emails before getting started with my jobs of the day. Each day I work on my objectives and other tasks I've been given. I like to organise my day by blocking my calendar out for each task I have to complete. This helps me work in a timely fashion and keep up with everything I have to do. I will then make my way to any meetings I may have. These can be in the office, or online via Skype or Teams. Top tip: take a notebook to every meeting and jot down any questions you may have.

As an apprentice, it is likely you take part in meetings where you don't understand things said. That is absolutely fine and the best thing to do is ask. This will help widen your knowledge and understanding of your role. When it gets to lunch time, this is when I head to the main canteen to catch up with other apprentices. It is important you are getting to see your apprentice friends during the week so you can catch up and spend time with one another. Some lunches we like to go on a walk of the site to stretch our legs and get some fresh air, and other times we will go out of site to grab a quick bite to eat. When I get back from my lunch break, the days consists of more independent work, meetings and networking with the people around me, before heading back to the station for my commute home.

Why did you choose a degree apprenticeship instead of going to university?

A degree apprenticeship has so many benefits. You are working, learning, and getting paid! With the level-4 business management scheme I am on, I get to experience seven different areas of the business over the four years. This will give me a wide scope of experience and will help me understand what job role I would like to end up with after completing my apprenticeship. Another benefit of this scheme in terms of university work is that it is all assessed on coursework and not exams. This is a huge benefit for me as I am the type of person who isn't very comfortable with the process of exams. The degree apprenticeship at Rolls-Royce is a wonderful option and has really helped me grow my confidence. This is why I chose to do a degree apprenticeship rather than going to university.

How do you balance studying while working?

Balancing studying while working was a big question I had before I started my apprenticeship. We get six hours a week to do university work. I usually take Fridays off work and spend the day doing it. Our assignments have longer due dates which really helps and means that I hardly ever have to use my weekends or weekday evenings doing university work. It can be easy to see these longs deadlines as a way to not get started on assignment work right away, but it is important to work on this every week, so it doesn't all pile up right before the deadline. All of my lecturers for first year have been extremely knowledgeable and very accommodating. We have a personal tutor who is there to support us during the four years. Mine is Sam, who is extremely helpful and is always available to talk about any issues I may have with university.

Any advice for someone thinking about a degree apprenticeship?

- Keep your options open, if you are not sure, apply to both university and an apprenticeship. You can take your time to decide what option is best for you.

- Ask around. Don't be afraid to ask any questions you may have. This will only help you understand the scheme more and help make your final decision.

- Learn from your application process. The different stages in the application process and interviews are all great experience whether you get the role or not. Be sure to ask for feedback from your interview to help you understand how to improve and what you did well.

Being a degree apprentice: comment by Ella Ragsdale

A day in the life

A typical day varies from placement to placement. Some days will be spent addressing emergent issues to resolve problems that are preventing production and delivery of components. Other longer ongoing tasks are balanced with these. Prioritising work is a skill that is developed quickly. Other areas of the business, such as research and development, do not have the emergent issues faced by production teams and projects are planned and longer in length. The apprenticeship is an ideal time to gain experience in these different areas and get a feel for where you thrive.

As an apprentice the tasks you complete must be documented as evidence towards your apprenticeship. Writing up evidence must be balanced alongside work to ensure the evidence is strong without impacting other work outputs. Apprentices also have regular meetings with assessors and apprentice managers to ensure progress is on track and that any issues are raised and addressed.

Communicating with different departments is a key part of the day job as an engineering apprentice. There are team meetings to attend to update the wider team on progress of different work packages. These may be weekly or daily, depending on the team. Team meetings may be sessions where the expertise in the team is shared to address a task collectively. I personally learn a lot from speaking to more experienced engineers and operators when discussing ongoing work packages.

During term time, I attend university one day a week. I like how university splits my week into two short sections, and it is a great time to catch up with other apprentices. Other daily tasks might include completing a training course, these can be delivered in a variety of ways including online and in person.

Why did you choose a degree apprenticeship instead of going to university?

I always wanted to do an apprenticeship rather than university, as I wanted the work experience and university never greatly appealed to me. Apprenticeships are a fantastic opportunity to gain experience and build a strong grounding for the rest of your career – something university alone does not offer.

The degree apprenticeship is the perfect blend of working and learning for me. I found I learn best by applying the knowledge at work. The degree apprenticeship with Rolls-Royce also offered two additional qualifications (NVQ level 2 and NVQ level 4 in engineering) that are not otherwise offered by the university route.

I also didn't know what discipline of engineering I wanted to work in. The degree apprenticeship is the perfect opportunity for me to gain experience in various engineering teams in the business before choosing where to continue my career.

How do you balance studying while working?

I personally am too tired by the end of a workday to work on university assignments. Hence, I make sure to relax in the evenings and spend my weekends completing assignments. I make sure that I stay on top of assignments throughout the university term, starting them as soon as possible. Completing assignments last minute whilst working full time is just not possible, but I find this a good motivator to start assignments early.

Exams tend to be a week or two after assignment deadlines. I accept that these will be busy times and personal time is limited. It is important to prioritise how you spend personal time to maintain relationships with friends and family. I always remind myself that the busy time is only twice a year and I make the most of my personal time throughout the rest of the year.

Any advice for someone thinking about a degree apprenticeship?

- If university doesn't seem right for you, a degree apprenticeship may be the way forward. That was definitely the case for me and I've not looked back once.

- Do what you find exciting and motivating. I think the most important thing about a job is finding it enjoyable and rewarding. It will also naturally help your career and personal development.

- Have a part-time job. No matter what industry, a part-time job will give you valuable skills, such as communication, multitasking, thinking on your feet, self-discipline and time management. All of these apply to the engineering industry. The work will also give you valuable experiences to talk about in interviews, especially discussing problems that you encountered and how you addressed them.

Graduating as a degree apprentice: comment by Alexia Williams

I pursued an engineering degree apprenticeship after completing my A-levels in maths, physics and product design. I'm now in a full-time role as a deployed lifecycle engineer, where I contribute to the operational lifecycle of engines.

Among my apprenticeship highlights, outward bound stands out, it instilled in me a sense of resilience, teamwork and problem-solving skills. Another was the opportunity to gain exposure to various teams and business functions through placement rotations, broadening my understanding of the business.

During my last placement, I completed a dissertation project that aimed at extending the lifespan of engines used by a military operator within the Russia-Ukraine war. Through this, I demonstrated Rolls-Royce's adaptability and commitment to supporting customers in critical situations.

A significant aspect of my apprenticeship involved participating in STEM events, where I shared my experiences and encouraged young individuals, especially girls, to pursue careers in engineering. Additionally, I took on the role of team lead at the Royal International Air Tattoo in 2022, showcasing my leadership abilities and contributing to the success of the event. I dedicated over a hundred hours to STEM initiatives in 2022, aiming to promote apprenticeships. My efforts were acknowledged when I was awarded STEM Ambassador of the Year 2022 in the South West.

In 2023, I was honoured to be a finalist for prestigious awards, such as the Royal Aeronautical Society Young Pioneer of the Year, Enginuity Degree Apprentice of the Year, Multicultural Apprentice Awards Engineering and Manufacturing Apprentice of the Year. These awards alongside achieving a first in my BEng aerospace engineering degree testify to my dedication and hard work put in throughout the four years.

Overall, my engineering degree apprenticeship has provided me with a robust educational foundation, valuable professional experiences, and numerous achievements that have shaped me into a skilled and accomplished young engineer.

CONCLUSION

Applying for degree apprenticeships is competitive. You will complete more than one application. The key to success is preparation. Use the steps in this book to guide you in completing your applications and the selection processes. The more time you invest in preparing and researching the company, the better chance you have.

Competing for a degree apprenticeship requires skills and attributes in addition to your academics. Engaging in extracurricular activities helps you build a wider set of skills and there are so many ways to develop these skills through school, volunteering or even taking on roles at home. The important fact is to allocate time outside of your academics to ensure you are building these additional skills.

SOURCES

Department for Business, Innovation and Skills, press statement (2015), 'Government rolls out flagship degree apprenticeships': gov.uk/government/news

UCAS / Sutton Trust (2023), *Where next? What influences the choices of would be apprentices?*: ucas.com

Sutton Trust, apprenticeships as a priority: suttontrust.com/ourpriorities/apprenticeships

Department for Education, education hub (2023), 'Medical doctor apprenticeships: everything you need to know': educationhub.blog.gov.uk

UCAS, news and insights (2023), 'UCAS launches new apprenticeships service as demand hits all time high': ucas.com

UCAS, news and insights (2023), 'Apprenticeship interest could hit half a million by 2030': ucas.com

www.ingramcontent.com/pod-product-compliance
Lightning Source LLC
Chambersburg PA
CBHW060612080526
44585CB00013B/796